The 99 Strongest Banks in America
And Why it Matters
John Truman Wolfe
2017

ISBN #: 978-1-387-41841-1

Table of Contents

INTRODUCTION

In the great John Schlesinger film, *Marathon Man*, Lawrence Olivier—playing Dr. Christian Szell, the Nazi war criminal dentist who tortured Jews in the concentration camps—kidnapped "Babe" Levy, played by Dustin Hoffman, and has him strapped to a chair.

In one of the most nerve-racking scenes in American cinema, Zell tortures Babe by repeatedly inserting a metal dental pick into a cavity in one of Babe's teeth.

Babe screams in unbearable agony while Zell (who is trying to determine if it is safe for him to recover some diamonds he stole from Auschwitz Jews) periodically asks Babe in a calmly evil tone, "Is it safe?"

Babe, who has no idea why Zell has abducted him or what diamonds he is talking about, alternatively answers "Yes" and "No," frantically trying to avoid another excruciating probe. Zell never gets a real answer and continues the torture until Babe is rescued by a U.S. government spy named Janeway, played by William Devane, who is also trying to get his corrupt hands on the diamonds.

But consider for a moment Zell asking the question to Jamie Diamond, the billionaire Chairman of JP Morgan Chase, the largest bank in the U.S., about the country's banking system - "Is it safe?" It would only take one nerve-shattering probe into a cavity for the Bitcoin-hating Chase Chairman to scream, "No. It's not safe."

And there you would have the truth of it.

Why is this the truth?

And if it is the truth, what does one do about it?

It is the truth because banking—in the U.S. and globally—has devolved into a colossal Vegas-like casino and bankers have become the ultimate "whale" gamblers.

The global banking system today has an estimated $1.2 quadrillion dollars in a kind of monetary heroin called derivatives.*

The figure is mind-numbing, but just to give you a sense of the size of this madness, here it is with the appropriate number of zeroes (15): $1,200,000,000,000,000.

Or, it may be more entertaining if you think of it this way: If you had a job that paid you $1,000 per second, it would take more than 31 years for you to earn $1 trillion.

A quadrillion is 1,000 trillion.

It's a big number. And I repeat, there are now $1.2 quadrillion dollars in derivatives held by financial institutions in the U.S. and abroad.

*What is a derivative? A derivative is a financial instrument, a security (like a stock or bond) that derives its value from some underlying asset. The most recognizable example of derivatives are the so-called mortgage-backed securities of the 2008 Global Financial Crisis infamy. Mortgage-backed securities are financial instruments that are packages of mortgages. They are not the actual mortgages themselves, they are the package, if you will, which is a security, containing the mortgages within it.

The mortgage-backed security derives its value from the income generated by the mortgages contained therein.

While there are some derivatives that serve a useful function in today's rodeo world of finance and investment, more than 70% of the $1.2 quadrillion are a kind of security called "interest rate swaps."

Interest rate swaps are... please pay attention because this is one of the most vital functions of banking today, it's what some banks do with your deposits ...bets.

Kind of makes you feel warm all over, doesn't it? Banks (not all, but larger ones) use your deposits to bet on the direction of interest rates.

For the sake of example, B of A thinks the rate on Greek bonds is going down, Deutsche Bank thinks the rate is going up. They structure an agreement that is a bet on which way the rate will go. The bet is a derivative called an interest rate swap.

Now, here's what's wild: others bet on the BofA/Deutsche Bank bet, and then others bet on those bets, and then others bet on the bets of the bets and this bizarre casino pyramids to infinity. Well, not quite infinity, just to approximately $840 trillion.

Isn't that special?

In the U.S., banks hold an estimated $250 trillion in derivatives. Here's a comparative: The gross domestic product of the United States is $16.6 trillion. Got it? In the U.S., the digital, smoke and mirrors, Mary Poppins derivatives market is 16 times larger than the real production of the entire country.

So, if Zell, dental probe at the ready, had asked his question to Jamie Diamond, whose bank carries $52 **trillion** dollars worth of derivatives, he would have said, "No."

Jamie is not alone. Of the $250 trillion in derivatives in U.S. banks, 92% are held by just 5 banks (These banks, by the way, control a significant percentage of all banking assets in the U.S.).

Take a look.

Citigroup
Total Assets: $1,800,967,000,000 (more than 1.8 trillion dollars)
Total Exposure To Derivatives: $55,624,082,000,000 (more than $55 trillion dollars)
JPMorgan Chase
Total Assets: $2,423,808,000,000 (about $2.4 trillion dollars)
Total Exposure To Derivatives: $52,352,138,000,000 (more than $52 trillion dollars)
Goldman Sachs
Total Assets: $878,102,000,000 (less than a trillion dollars)
Total Exposure To Derivatives: $52,257,748,000,000 (more than $52 trillion dollars)
Bank Of America
Total Assets: $2,188,633,000,000 (a little bit more than $2.1 trillion dollars)
Total Exposure To Derivatives: $42,998,807,000,000 (almost $43 trillion dollars)
Morgan Stanley
Total Assets: $807,497,000,000 (less than a trillion dollars)
Total Exposure To Derivatives: $28,281,106, 000,000 (more than $31 trillion dollars).

You see why Jamie would have confessed?

What happens when the derivatives bubble bursts? (And if you think this financial Hindenburg will continue to float without someone sticking a pin it, I invite you to take a quick review of 2008 when it was just some mortgage-backed securities that turned sour—small potatoes compared to the 250 trillion dollar crap game now in progress.)

When the derivatives market implodes, these big banks are going to go under, right?

Well…not really. The Godfather protects *The Family*.

The Godfather of the Global Financial Mafia—and trust me the metaphor is apt—is a bank in Basel, Switzerland called the Bank for International Settlements—known to other members of the mob as the BIS.

Haven't heard of it? Neither have most people.

But the Bank for International Settlements is the most powerful financial institution in the world.

The BIS is a universe unto itself, where they make their own rules and play their own games. Though based in Switzerland, Swiss law does not affect it; its employees are immune from prosecution; their property is inviolate, and they even have their own law enforcement forces on premises.

It is the central banker's central bank. The sixty central banks of the world: the U.S. Federal Reserve Bank, the People's Bank of China, the central banks of Russia, Saudi Arabia, Mexico, Germany, Japan, Italy, Canada, ad infinitum, are all members of the Bank for International Settlements.

The membership of this elite, private, ex-Nazi bank represent 95% of the world's GDP.

I will put modesty aside for a moment and strongly encourage you to read my book, *The Coming Financial Crisis, A Look Behind the Wizard's Curtain*, which exposes the machinations of the BIS in much greater detail—I name names, dates, and places.
http://www.amazon.com/Coming-Financial-Crisis-Wizards-Curtain/dp/0996968644/ref=sr_1_1?ie=UTF8&qid=1459935146&sr=8-1&keywords=john+truman+wolfe

For now, you should understand that it is the BIS that dictates to the central banks of the world, who controls the economies of their respective countries. Virtually all of these countries are bankrupt, so you can see how that has been working out for them.

Seeing that the major banks of the world were buried in this fiscal anthrax, the Godfather devised a plan. The plan goes by the name of "Bail In" and here is how it works: Failing banks are able to confiscate the money in depositors' accounts and convert that money to stock in the failing bank.

Go ahead. Read that again. The words won't change.

An entity called the Financial Stability Board, created in April 2009, which operates inside of The Bank for International Settlements, devised this scheme. Bail-in policy was formally implemented for all European banks on January 1, 2016. http://www.activistpost.com/2015/12/january-1-2016-the-new-bank-bail-in-system-goes-into-effect-in-europe.html. (The first European bank was subjected to the new bail in procedure in early April, 2016. http://www.zerohedge.com/news/2016-04-10/austria-just-announced-54-haircut-senior-creditors-first-bail-under-new-european-rul).

Canada implemented the bail-in procedure for it banks on March 22, 2016.

http://www.zerohedge.com/news/2016-03-22/its-official-canadian-bank-depositors-are-now-risk-bail-ins

The FDIC and the Bank of England issued a memo as far back as 2012 detailing how bail-ins would be administered in the U.S. and England. There have not been any formal bail-ins in the U.S. yet, but the foundation is laid and the operating rules have been set forth.

http://www.bankofengland.co.uk/publications/Documents/news/2012/nr156.pdf

You with me? Less than half a dozen major banks in the country, which control a huge percentage of the country's banking assets, are buried in malignant securities. Sooner or later, they will eat the host. However, when a banking crisis results, these terminally ill banks will have the ability to "save themselves" by confiscating depositors' money and converting it into bank stock to recapitalize themselves.

This is like something out of a Stephen King novel—a horror story about banks that become vampires and suck the life from their depositors' accounts. Except, it's happening "as we speak."

Will FDIC insurance protect a depositor in a bail-in scenario? One presumes so. But there are two points to consider here. One, the joint FDIC / Bank of England memo on bail-ins makes no mention of deposit insurance whatsoever. Just seems odd.

The other factor is this: When one of these giant banks goes down and the dominoes start to cascade into a banking bankruptcy freefall to other banks, the FDIC insurance fund has about $67 billion; there is about $11 trillion deposited in U.S. banks. It is not all insured, but in a real banking crisis, the FDIC insurance fund would vanish in the blink of an eye.

Still, there is one more piece to this puzzle: According to U.S. bankruptcy laws, derivatives are considered secured creditors and have first claim on the bank's assets; depositors are unsecured creditors and have a junior claim on remaining assets.

Did you know that when you deposit money in the bank, it is technically and legally no longer "your" money? The money belongs to the bank. You are a creditor. They owe you the money as if you laid the carpet in the lobby, but the money belongs to the bank—you are not only just a creditor, you are an <u>unsecured</u> creditor.

So, do you now see why Jamie was screaming "No!"? Because the banks are pregnant with toxic derivatives, and when the derivatives market implodes (think 2008 cubed), the big banks will make themselves whole by taking depositors' money using the bail-in procedure, and just to ensure those derivative investments are safeguarded, they are protected by the bankruptcy laws with first claim on the bank's assets.

When Jamie screams, "No. It's not safe," he means not for the ordinary depositor. And now you can see why.

So what do you do?

My suggestion is if you are banking at any of the large "money center" banks, those listed above and others I will reference below, I would move your accounts to a smaller independent bank (a bank under $50 billion in assets). And that is why I have conducted the research and written this small book—to give you banking alternatives from those banks that the BIS and the banking elite no longer call "Too big to fail." They quit using that term because of the negative PR it received during the last financial crisis. They are now labeled with sophisticated-sounding banker babel—Globally Systematic Important Financial Institutions (G-SIFI).

These megabanks—G-SIFIs—are the banks that have both extensive U.S. and international operations.

Some of the U.S. banks in this category: Bank of America, J.P Morgan Chase, Wells Fargo, Citigroup (Citibank), Goldman Sachs and Morgan Stanley.

Those that simply have U.S. operations are called D-SIFBs— Domestically-Systematically Important Banks. A few of the banks on this list that you might recognize include: Capital One, HSBC, Regions, SunTrust, US Bank, Union Bank.

A list of both can be found here.
https://en.wikipedia.org/wiki/List_of_systemically_important_banks

However, I have done extensive research and located several dozen independent banks across the United States that have exceptionally strong financial statements and would be much better prepared to weather a major banking crisis than the vast majority of other banks in the country.

Importantly, being under $50 billion in assets, they are not in the category of "Systematically Important Domestic Banks," and not likely to be subject to the FDIC's bail-in carnage.

While neither I nor anyone can guarantee that any particular bank will survive such a crisis, an analysis of the banks I have listed below demonstrates fiscal prudence on the part of the bank's management resulting in strong financial statements, which means better protection for their depositors.

One can be drowned in the waves of statistics that regulators regurgitate when conducting an analysis of the strength of a bank. And surely there will be those who will object to the statistics I consider the most important or will argue that others should be used.

Perhaps. But I'm an old-fashioned banker, and the measurements that I include here are the ones I deem most vital to survival. It is not that other statistics might not be important or that other systems could not be used—but some of these "systems" place undue emphasis on aspects of a bank's performance that put the depositor at risk.

Here's one example, a bank rating site that I reviewed had given a particular bank a 5-star rating (the highest) when the bank's loan to deposit ratio was over 100%.

Plain English: One measurement of the bank's strength is the bank's liquidity. To calculate the bank's liquidity, we determine the loan to deposit ratio. If a bank has $1,000,000 in deposits and has lent out $700,000 of those deposits in loans—the loan to deposit ratio would be 70%.

A general rule of thumb is that a 70% loan to deposit ratio is a good conservative target for most banks. As a bank moves beyond that (seeking to generate more income by lending a larger and larger percentage of its deposits), they become less and less liquid and fewer deposits are available to the demands of their customers should they be made. Over 80% is generally considered risky.

The bank listed in the rating site in the example above had not only lent out all of their customer's deposits but had borrowed money to lend out more. I'm not sure what these guys are smoking, but this is reckless banking and I was shocked that the rating site had given it 5 stars.

All of which is to say, I use my own—conservative—system of assessing a bank's strength.

I look at the size of the bank, which is determined by its total assets.

I review the bank's bottom line and ensure it is profitable. This isn't rocket science, a bank has to make a profit or it will have to close its doors. But some who assess the strength of banks, assign an altered importance to the institution's profitability to the exclusion of other factors. Banks have to be profitable, no question, but other factors are also key. So, I assess the bank's profitability along with my evaluation.

A vital aspect of a bank's financial health is the institution's loan portfolio. Do they make sound loans or don't they? Too many bad loans and the briefcase-toting droids from the FDIC show up and shut the place down.

One way to measure the quality of the loan portfolio is to determine what percent of their loans are "not performing." Banks have to report this figure to regulators. Non-performing loans are those that are 90 days or more past due. There are a few ways one can measure this statistic, but here is a simple one.

One can evaluate what percent the non-performing loans are of the bank's overall assets. You will notice in the list of "Best Banks" below, that in every case, the non-performing loans are less than 1% of the bank's assets.

There is another way to measure how likely a bank is to be adversely affected by its non-performing loans.

Banks set money aside in a special account to cover possible loan losses. You know, the borrower skips town with the new Caddy and the cocktail waitress from the Lazy J Saloon, or the sale of a foreclosed property did not cover the loan balance. The bank allocates money to cover the loss or pending loss.

This account is called a loan loss reserve account.

One can see if bad loans are going to impact the bank's profitability and strength by reviewing how much the bank has in the loan loss reserve account as a percentage of the non-performing loans. For example, the bank has $500,000 in non-performing loans on the books. They have

$750,000 in the loan loss reserve accounts to cover bad loans. Thus, they have 150% coverage of the bad loans. Decent coverage.

If they only had $400,000 in the loan loss reserve account and $500,000 in non-performing loans, they would just have 80% coverage of the bad loans.

Less than 100% is risky. The higher the percentage of coverage the better.

It is important to know how strong the bank's capital is. Capital is also called equity. It is the "ownership" value of the bank. Capital, in its most basic form, is the amount of money invested in the bank plus the accumulated profits that the bank retains—profits retained, not paid out in dividends to shareholders.

In short, equity is the difference between the bank's assets and liabilities. A bank has $1,000,000,000 dollars in assets (cash, investments, loans they have made, buildings) and $850,000,000 in liabilities (accounts payables, customer's deposits, etc.). The equity, the difference between the assets and the liabilities in this example, is $150,000,000 or 15% of the assets. Theoretically, if all the assets were liquidated and all the liabilities paid, there would be $150,000,000 remaining. This is the net ownership of the bank and is also the cushion that protects depositors.

The Bank for International Settlement, which sets the capital requirements for banks, has different nuances they spray on this, but the current minimum capital requirement for a bank is 8%. The capital of the bank must be 8% of the assets. In the example above, the bank has almost twice the statutory minimum required.

Those are the key measurements I review in determining the strength of a bank: asset size, loan to deposit ratio, profitability, portfolio quality, and capital.

Using these guidelines, the following is a list of banks I consider strong. These are based on the statistics reported as of March 31, 2016. These figures come from one of the two main bank rating sites, www.bankrate.com or www.bauerfinancial.com (which sometimes differ slightly), and my own evaluation.

THE 99 STRONGEST BANKS

The banks are organized by states.

BANK STATISTICS

ALABAMA

Cheaha Bank
1320 Highway Drive
Oxford, Alabama 36203
www.cheahabank.com
Assets: $197 million
Loans: $109 million
Deposits: $165 million
Loan to deposit ratio: 66%
Profitability: nicely above average
Nonperforming loans as a percent of assets: 0.22%
Loan-loss reserves as a percent of nonperforming loans: 877%
Equity as a percent of assets: 12%

First Bank of Boaz
124 S. Main Street
Boaz, Alabama 35957
www.firstbankofboaz.com
Assets: $205 million
Loans: $51 million
Deposits: $145 million
Loan to deposit ratio: 76%
Profitability: average
Nonperforming loans as a percent of assets: 0.01%
Loan-loss reserves as a percent of nonperforming loans: 519%
Equity as a percent of assets: 37%

First Citizens Bank
100 West Third Street
Luverne, Alabama 36049
www.fcbl.com
Assets: $233 million
Loans: $110 million
Deposits: $190 million
Loan to deposit ratio: 67%
Profitability: average
Nonperforming loans as a percent of assets: 0.37%
Loan-loss reserves as a percent of nonperforming loans: 1,375%
Equity as a percent of assets: 18%

First National Bank
341 Military Street South
Hamilton, Alabama 35570
www.fnbhamilton.com
Assets: $289 million
Loans: $119 million
Deposits: $242 million
Loan to deposit ratio: 49%
Profitability: average
Nonperforming loans as a percent of assets: 0.15%
Loan-loss reserves as a percent of nonperforming loans: 441%
Equity as a percent of assets: 16%

Pinnacle Bank
1811 2nd Avenue
Jasper, Alabama 35502
www.pinnaclebanc.com
Assets: $224 million
Loans: $85 million
Deposits: $190 million
Loan to deposit ratio: 45%
Profitability: average

Nonperforming loans as a percent of assets: 0.08%
Loan-loss reserves as a percent of nonperforming loans: 861%
Equity as a percent of assets: 13%

ALASKA

First National Bank Alaska
646 West Fourth Avenue
Anchorage, Alaska 99510
www.fnbalaska.com
Assets: $3,617 million
Loans: $1,561 million
Deposits: $2,430 million
Loan to deposit ratio: 64%
Profitability: average
Nonperforming loans as a percent of assets: 0.53%
Loan-loss reserves as a percent of nonperforming loans: 473%
Equity as a percent of assets: 14%

ARKANSAS

Citizens Bank & Trust Company
3110 Alma Highway
Van Buren, Arkansas 72957
www.cbankandtrust.com
Assets: $375 million
Loans: $221 million
Deposits: $325 million
Loan to deposit ratio: 68%
Profitability: above average
Nonperforming loans as a percent of assets: 0.39%
Loan-loss reserves as a percent of nonperforming loans: 313%
Equity as a percent of assets: 13%

DeWitt Bank and Trust Company
215 South Jefferson Street
DeWitt, Arkansas 72042
www.dewittbankandtrust.com
Assets: $119 million
Loans: $34 million
Deposits: $90 million
Loan to deposit ratio: 38%
Profitability: slightly below average
Nonperforming loans as a percent of assets: 0.48%
Loan-loss reserves as a percent of nonperforming loans: 9,415%
Equity as a percent of assets: 20%

First Security Bank
314 North Spring
Searcy, Arkansas 72143
www.fsbank.com
Assets: $4,983 million
Loans: $1,977 million
Deposits: $3,595 million
Loan to deposit ratio: 55%
Profitability: above average
Nonperforming loans as a percent of assets: 0.43%
Loan-loss reserves as a percent of nonperforming loans: 473%
Equity as a percent of assets: 16%

Peoples Bank
1120 South Rock Street
Sheridan, Arkansas 72150
www.peoplesbankar.com
Assets: $136 million
Loans: $68 million
Deposits: $116 million
Loan to deposit ratio: 58%
Profitability: average

Nonperforming loans as a percent of assets: 0.11%
Loan-loss reserves as a percent of nonperforming loans: 694%
Equity as a percent of assets: 14%

CALIFORNIA

Bank of Hemet
3715 Sunnyside Drive
Riverside, California 92506
www.bankofhemet.com
Assets: $656 million
Loans: $404 million
Deposits: $594 million
Loan to deposit ratio: 68%
Profitability: highly profitable
Nonperforming loans as a percent of assets: 0.00
Loan-loss reserves as a percent of nonperforming loans: not applicable
Equity as a percent of assets: 9%

Citizens Business Bank
701 North Haven
Ontario, California 91764
www.cbbank.com
Assets: $7,915 million
Loans: $4,114 million
Deposits: $6,233 million
Loan to deposit ratio: 66%
Profitability: slightly above average
Nonperforming loans as a percent of assets: 0.31%
Loan-loss reserves as a percent of nonperforming loans: 324%
Equity as a percent of assets: 12%

Farmers and Merchants Bank of Long Beach

302 Pine Avenue
Long Beach, California 90802
www.fmb.com
Assets: $6,221 million
Loans: $3,277 million
Deposits: $4,756 million
Loan to deposit ratio: 69%
Profitability: average
Nonperforming loans as a percent of assets: 0.04%
Loan-loss reserves as a percent of nonperforming loans: 3,262%
Equity as a percent of assets: 14%

Five Star Bank
6810 Five Star Boulevard, Suite 100
Rocklin, California 95677
www.fivestarbank.com
Assets: $810 million
Loans: $558 million
Deposits: $743 million
Loan to deposit ratio: 75%
Profitability: highly profitable
Nonperforming loans as a percent of assets: 0.01%
Loan-loss reserves as a percent of nonperforming loans: 8,622%
Equity as a percent of assets: 8%

COLORADO

Collegiate Peaks Bank
105 Centennial Plaza
Buena Vista, Colorado 81211
www.collegiatepeaksbank.com
Assets: $412 million
Loans: $267 million
Deposits: $348 million
Loan to deposit ratio: 77%

Profitability: average
Nonperforming loans as a percent of assets: 0.03 %
Loan-loss reserves as a percent of nonperforming loans: 3,058%
Equity as a percent of assets: 12%

Solera National Bank
319 South Sheridan Boulevard
Lakewood, Colorado 80226
www.solerabank.com
Assets: $141 million
Loans: $78 million
Deposits: $116 million
Loan to deposit ratio: 68%
Profitability: average
Nonperforming loans as a percent of assets: 0.00%
Loan-loss reserves as a percent of nonperforming loans: not applicable
Equity as a percent of assets: 14%

FLORIDA

First Colony Bank of Florida
711 North Orlando Avenue
Maitland, Florida 32794
www.firstcolonybank.net
Assets: $203 million
Loans: $122 million
Deposits: $182 million
Loan to deposit ratio: 67%
Profitability: above average
Nonperforming loans as a percent of assets: 0.03%
Loan-loss reserves as a percent of nonperforming loans: 3,925%
Equity as a percent of assets: 10%

Hillsboro Bank

509 West Alexander Street
Plant City, Florida 33566
www.hillsborobank.com
Assets: $119 million
Loans: $55 million
Deposits: $101 million
Loan to deposit ratio: 54%
Profitability: average
Nonperforming loans as a percent of assets: 0.00%
Loan-loss reserves as a percent of nonperforming loans: not applicable
Equity as a percent of assets: 14%

IDAHO

Bank of Commerce
3113 South 25th East
Ammon, Idaho 83406
www.bankofcommerce.org
Assets: $1,034 million
Loans: $616 million
Deposits: $872 million
Loan to deposit ratio: 71%
Profitability: average
Nonperforming loans as a percent of assets: 0.64%
Loan-loss reserves as a percent of nonperforming loans: $187 million
Equity as a percent of assets: 15%

ILLINOIS

Farmers National Bank
114 West 3rd Street
Prophetstown, Illinois 61277
www.farmersnationalbank.com
Assets: $552 million

Loans: $283 million
Deposits: $417 million
Loan to deposit ratio: 68%
Profitability: average
Nonperforming loans as a percent of assets: 0.52%
Loan-loss reserves as a percent of nonperforming loans: 466%
Equity as a percent of assets: 15%

First National Bank in Taylorville
322 West Main Cross
Taylorville, Illinois 62568
www.fnbtaylorville.com
Assets: $201 million
Loans: $80 million
Deposits: $167 million
Loan to deposit ratio: 48%
Profitability: slightly above average
Nonperforming loans as a percent of assets: 0.31%
Loan-loss reserves as a percent of nonperforming loans: 180%
Equity as a percent of assets: 15%

First National Bank of Pana
306 South Locust Street
Pana, Illinois 62557
www.fnbpana.com
Assets: $174 million
Loans: $114 million
Deposits: $155 million
Loan to deposit ratio: 74%
Profitability: nicely above average
Nonperforming loans as a percent of assets: 0.16%
Loan-loss reserves as a percent of nonperforming loans: 507%
Equity as a percent of assets: 10%

First Trust and Savings Bank of Watseka

120 East Walnut Street
Watseka, Illinois 60970
http://www.ftsbank.com/
Assets: $237 million
Loans: $103 million
Deposits: $202 million
Loan to deposit ratio: 51%
Profitability: average
Nonperforming loans as a percent of assets: 0.16%
Loan-loss reserves as a percent of nonperforming loans: 493%
Equity as a percent of assets: 14%

Germantown Trust & Savings Bank
205 Germantown Road
Breese, Illinois 62230
www.gtsb.com
Assets: $352 million
Loans: $179 million
Deposits: $271 million
Loan to deposit ratio: 66%
Profitability: above average
Nonperforming loans as a percent of assets: 0.10%
Loan-loss reserves as a percent of nonperforming loans: 651%
Equity as a percent of assets: 14%

Rushville State Bank
100 East Lafayette Street
Rushville, Illinois 62681
www.rushvillestatebank.com
Assets: $101 million
Loans: $41 million
Deposits: $85 million
Loan to deposit ratio: 48%
Profitability: average
Nonperforming loans as a percent of assets: 0.16%

Loan-loss reserves as a percent of nonperforming loans: 287%
Equity as a percent of assets: 14%

Soy Capital Bank and Trust Company
1501 East Eldorado
Decatur, Illinois 62521
www.soybank.com
Assets: $408 million
Loans: $202 million
Deposits: $295 million
Loan to deposit ratio: 68%
Profitability: slightly below average
Nonperforming loans as a percent of assets: 0.24%
Loan-loss reserves as a percent of nonperforming loans: 502%
Equity as a percent of assets: 17%

Teutopolis State Bank
106 East Main Street
Teutopolis, Illinois 62467
www.teutopolisstatebank.com
Assets: $212 million
Loans: $110 million
Deposits: $184 million
Loan to deposit ratio: 60%
Profitability: average
Nonperforming loans as a percent of assets: 0.01%
Loan-loss reserves as a percent of nonperforming loans: 4,665%
Equity as a percent of assets: 13%

INDIANA

Merchants Bank of Indiana
11555 North Meridian Street, Suite 400
Carmel, Indiana 46032

www.merchantsbankofindiana.com
Assets: $2,468 million
Loans: $1,620 million
Deposits: $2,236 million
Loan to deposit ratio: 72%
Profitability: nicely above average
Nonperforming loans as a percent of assets: 0.04%
Loan-loss reserves as a percent of nonperforming loans: 719%
Equity as a percent of assets: 8%

IOWA

Bank First
115 North Vine
West Union, Iowa 52175
www.bank1stia.com
Assets: $126 million
Loans: $83 million
Deposits: $111 million
Loan to deposit ratio: 75%
Profitability: average
Nonperforming loans as a percent of assets: 0.04%
Loan-loss reserves as a percent of nonperforming loans: $2,237 million
Equity as a percent of assets: 11%

Citizens First National Bank
East 5th & Lake Avenue
Storm Lake, Iowa 50588
www.citizensfnb.com
Assets: $225 million
Loans: $116 million
Deposits: $202 million
Loan to deposit ratio: 58%
Profitability: nicely above average

Nonperforming loans as a percent of assets: 0.11%
Loan-loss reserves as a percent of nonperforming loans: 437%
Equity as a percent of assets: 10%

Citizens Savings Bank
101 Church Street
Spillville, Iowa 52168
www.bankingwithcsb.com
Assets: $104 million
Loans: $50 million
Deposits: $83 million
Loan to deposit ratio: 60%
Profitability: slightly above average
Nonperforming loans as a percent of assets: 0.23%
Loan-loss reserves as a percent of nonperforming loans: 311%
Equity as a percent of assets: 14%

Citizens State Bank
117 West 1st Street
Monticello, Iowa 52310
www.citizensstateonline.com
Assets: $377 million
Loans: $230 million
Deposits: $310 million
Loan to deposit ratio: 74%
Profitability: above average
Nonperforming loans as a percent of assets: 0.06%
Loan-loss reserves as a percent of nonperforming loans: 1,093%
Equity as a percent of assets: 12%

Community State Bank
1812 Highway Boulevard
Spencer, Iowa 51301
www.ecommunitybank.org
Assets: $146 million

Loans: $87 million
Deposits: $122 million
Loan to deposit ratio: 71%
Profitability: above average
Nonperforming loans as a percent of assets: 0.02%
Loan-loss reserves as a percent of nonperforming loans: 4,272%
Equity as a percent of assets: 11%

First Bank Hampton
211 1st Avenue Northwest
Hampton, Iowa 50441
www.firstbankhampton.com
Assets: $154 million
Loans: $87 million
Deposits: $135 million
Loan to deposit ratio: 35%
Profitability: above average
Nonperforming loans as a percent of assets: 0.14%
Loan-loss reserves as a percent of nonperforming loans: 4,533%
Equity as a percent of assets: 18%

First State Bank
1150 West First Street
Sumner, Iowa 50674
www.fsbsumner.com
Assets: $103 million
Loans: $52 million
Deposits: $73 million
Loan to deposit ratio: 71%
Profitability: slightly below average
Nonperforming loans as a percent of assets: 0.14 %
Loan-loss reserves as a percent of nonperforming loans: 1,069%
Equity as a percent of assets: 14%

Iowa State Bank

627 East Locust
Des Moines, Iowa 50309
www.iowastatebanks.com
Assets: $374 million
Loans: $147 million
Deposits: $302 million
Loan to deposit ratio: 49%
Profitability: slightly above average
Nonperforming loans as a percent of assets: 0.01%
Loan-loss reserves as a percent of nonperforming loans: 5,261%
Equity as a percent of assets: 16%

Iowa Trust and Savings Bank
200 North 10th
Centerville, Iowa 52544
www.itsb-iowa.com
Assets: $177 million
Loans: $83 million
Deposits: $135 million
Loan to deposit ratio: 61%
Profitability: above average
Nonperforming loans as a percent of assets: 0.16%
Loan-loss reserves as a percent of nonperforming loans: 346%
Equity as a percent of assets: 11%

Liberty Trust & Savings Bank
502 Eighth Avenue
Durant, Iowa 52747
www.mylibertytrust.com
Assets: $150 million
Loans: $70 million
Deposits: $114 million
Loan to deposit ratio: 62%
Profitability: slightly below average
Nonperforming loans as a percent of assets: 0.28%

Loan-loss reserves as a percent of nonperforming loans: 1,387%
Equity as a percent of assets: 18%

Midwest Heritage Bank FSB
West Des Moines, Iowa 50265
www.mhbank.com
Assets: $231 million
Loans: $151 million
Deposits: $200 million
Loan to deposit ratio: 76%
Profitability: average
Nonperforming loans as a percent of assets: 0.00%
Loan-loss reserves as a percent of nonperforming loans: not applicable
Equity as a percent of assets: 12%

New Albin Savings Bank
118 Main North East
New Albin, Iowa 52160
www.newalbinsavingsbank.com
Assets: $223 million
Loans: $62 million
Deposits: $171 million
Loan to deposit ratio: 36%
Profitability: average
Nonperforming loans as a percent of assets: 0.06%
Loan-loss reserves as a percent of nonperforming loans: 551%
Equity as a percent of assets: 18%

Security State Bank
231 1st Street East
Independence, Iowa 50644
www.ssbindee.com
Assets: $104 million
Loans: $45 million
Deposits: $82 million

Loan to deposit ratio: 55%
Profitability: average
Nonperforming loans as a percent of assets: 0.00%
Loan-loss reserves as a percent of nonperforming loans: 34,933%
Equity as a percent of assets: 13%

South Ottumwa Savings Bank
320 Church Street
Ottumwa, Iowa 52501
www.sosb-ia.com
Assets: $397 million
Loans: $173 million
Deposits: $315 million
Loan to deposit ratio: 55%
Profitability: average
Nonperforming loans as a percent of assets: 0.27%
Loan-loss reserves as a percent of nonperforming loans: 334%
Equity as a percent of assets: 13%

KANSAS

Farmers Bank & Trust
1017 Harrison
Great Bend, Kansas 67530
www.farmersbankks.com
Assets: $746 million
Loans: $269 million
Deposits: $500 million
Loan to deposit ratio: 54%
Profitability: above average
Nonperforming loans as a percent of assets: 1.15%
Loan-loss reserves as a percent of nonperforming loans: 361%
Equity as a percent of assets: 17%

Fidelity State Bank and Trust Company
510 North 2nd Avenue
Dodge City, Kansas 67801
www.fidelitybankdc.com
Assets: $174 million
Loans: $36 million
Deposits: $142 million
Loan to deposit ratio: 60%
Profitability: slightly below average
Nonperforming loans as a percent of assets: 0.21%
Loan-loss reserves as a percent of nonperforming loans: 363%
Equity as a percent of assets: 10%

First Bank
128 South Broadway
Sterling, Kansas 67579
www.first-bank.net
Assets: $132 million
Loans: $67 million
Deposits: $106 million
Loan to deposit ratio: 61%
Profitability: average
Nonperforming loans as a percent of assets: 0.09%
Loan-loss reserves as a percent of nonperforming loans: 294%
Equity as a percent of assets: 12%

First National Bank and Trust
225 State Street
Phillipsburg, Kansas 67661
www.agbank.com
Assets: $199 million
Loans: $120 million
Deposits: $166 million
Loan to deposit ratio: 73%
Profitability: average

Nonperforming loans as a percent of assets: 0.66%
Loan-loss reserves as a percent of nonperforming loans: 525%
Equity as a percent of assets: 16%

First State Bank & Trust Company of Larned
116 West 6th
Larned, Kansas 67550
www.fusion.bank
Assets: $140 million
Loans: $79 million
Deposits: $111 million
Loan to deposit ratio: 71%
Profitability: slightly above-average
Nonperforming loans as a percent of assets: 0.21%
Loan-loss reserves as a percent of nonperforming loans: 529%
Equity as a percent of assets: 12%

Flint Hills Bank
103 ½ North Main Street
Eskridge, Kansas 66423
www.flinthillsbank.com
Assets: $122 million
Loans: $66 million
Deposits: $105 million
Loan to deposit ratio: 62%
Profitability: above average
Nonperforming loans as a percent of assets: 0.32
Loan-loss reserves as a percent of nonperforming loans: 2,431%
Equity as a percent of assets: 12%

Peoples Bank and Trust Company
101 South Main
McPherson, Kansas 67460
www.peoplesbankonline.com
Assets: $446 million

Loans: $247 million
Deposits: $351 million
Loan to deposit ratio: 70%
Profitability: average
Nonperforming loans as a percent of assets: 0.22%
Loan-loss reserves as a percent of nonperforming loans: 485%
Equity as a percent of assets: 13%

KENTUCKY

Citizens Bank & Trust Company
201 East Main Street
Campbellsville, Kentucky 42718
www.cbtky.com
Assets: $210 million
Loans: $98 million
Deposits: $175 million
Loan to deposit ratio: 56%
Profitability: slightly below average
Nonperforming loans as a percent of assets: 0.19 %
Loan-loss reserves as a percent of nonperforming loans: 410%
Equity as a percent of assets: 16%

Commonwealth Community Bank, Inc.
830 South Main Street
Hartford, Kentucky 42347
www.cwcbankhb.com
Assets: $149 million
Loans: $38 million
Deposits: $120 million
Loan to deposit ratio: 32%
Profitability: average
Nonperforming loans as a percent of assets: 0.16%
Loan-loss reserves as a percent of nonperforming loans: 308%

Equity as a percent of assets: 15%

Jackson County Bank
1st & Main Street
McKee, Kentucky 40447
www.jacksoncobank.com
Assets: $132 million
Loans: $64 million
Deposits: $94 million
Loan to deposit ratio: 68%
Profitability: below average
Nonperforming loans as a percent of assets: 0.43%
Loan-loss reserves as a percent of nonperforming loans: 330%
Equity as a percent of assets: 26%

Springfield State Bank
125 East Main Street
Springfield, Kentucky 40069
www.springfieldstate.com
Assets: $301 million
Loans: $135 million
Deposits: $222 million
Loan to deposit ratio: 61%
Profitability: average
Nonperforming loans as a percent of assets: 0.17%
Loan-loss reserves as a percent of nonperforming loans: 419%
Equity as a percent of assets: 13%

LOUISIANA

Jonesboro State Bank
109 Jimmie Davis Blvd.
Jonesboro, LA 71251
www.jonesborostatebank.com

Assets: $209 million
Loans: $30 million
Deposits: $173 million
Loan to deposit ratio: 17%
Profitability: Above average
Nonperforming loans as a percent of assets: 0.50%
Loan-loss reserves as a percent of nonperforming loans: 79%
Equity as a percent of assets: 14%

MBL Bank
100 MBL Bank Drive
Minden, Louisiana 71058
www.mblbank.com
Assets: $320 million
Loans: $189 million
Deposits: $261 million
Loan to deposit ratio: 72%
Profitability: average
Nonperforming loans as a percent of assets: 0.12%
Loan-loss reserves as a percent of nonperforming loans: 487%
Equity as a percent of assets: 16%

MINNESOTA

Eagle Bank
2 South Franklin
Glenwood, Minnesota 56334
www.eaglebankmn.com
Assets: $142 million
Loans: $82 million
Deposits: $123 million
Loan to deposit ratio: 67%
Profitability: average
Nonperforming loans as a percent of assets: 0.13%

Loan-loss reserves as a percent of nonperforming loans: 2,514%
Equity as a percent of assets: 13%

Granite Falls Bank
702 Prentice St.
Granite Falls, Minnesota 56241
www.granitefallsbank.com
Assets: $190 million
Loans: $67 million
Deposits: $142 million
Loan to deposit ratio: 48%
Profitability: nicely above average
Nonperforming loans as a percent of assets: 0.07%
Loan-loss reserves as a percent of nonperforming loans: 570%
Equity as a percent of assets: 11%

Liberty Bank Minnesota
111 7th Avenue South
Saint Cloud, Minnesota 56301
www.libertybankmn.com
Assets: 198 million
Loans: 98 million
Deposits: 174 million
Loan to deposit ratio: 57%
Profitability: nicely above average
Nonperforming loans as a percent of assets: 0.00%
Loan-loss reserves as a percent of nonperforming loans: not applicable
Equity as a percent of assets: 12%

North American Banking Company
2230 Albert Street
Roseville, Minnesota 55113
www.nabankco.com
Assets: $403 million
Loans: $274 million

Deposits: $348 million
Loan to deposit ratio: 79%
Profitability: above average
Nonperforming loans as a percent of assets: 0.02%
Loan-loss reserves as a percent of nonperforming loans: 4,781%
Equity as a percent of assets: 9%

State Bank of New Prague
1101 First Street SE
New Prague, Minnesota 56071
www.statebankofnewprague.com
Assets: $111 million
Loans: $38 million
Deposits: $94 million
Loan to deposit ratio: 41%
Profitability: slightly above average
Nonperforming loans as a percent of assets: 0.23%
Loan-loss reserves as a percent of nonperforming loans: 303%
Equity as a percent of assets: 14%

MISSISSIPPI

Commerce Bank
306 South Cass Street
Corinth, Mississippi 38835
www.commercebk.com
Assets: $103 million
Loans: $69 million
Deposits: $90 million
Loan to deposit ratio: 77%
Profitability: above average
Nonperforming loans as a percent of assets: 0.25%
Loan-loss reserves as a percent of nonperforming loans: 802%
Equity as a percent of assets: 12%

First National Bank of Clarksdale
402 East Second Street
Clarksdale, Mississippi 38614
www.fnbclarksdale.com
Assets: $362 million
Loans: $203 million
Deposits: $298 million
Loan to deposit ratio: 68%
Profitability: average
Nonperforming loans as a percent of assets: 0.15%
Loan-loss reserves as a percent of nonperforming loans: 1,684%
Equity as a percent of assets: 12%

Jefferson Bank
600 Main St
Rosedale, MS 38769
www.thejeffersonbank.com
Assets: $101 million
Loans: $60 million
Deposits: $82 million
Loan to deposit ratio: 72%
Profitability: average
Nonperforming loans as a percent of assets: 0.13%
Loan-loss reserves as a percent of nonperforming loans: 1,113%
Equity as a percent of assets: 18%

MISSOURI

Bank of Old Monroe
2100 Highway C
Old Monroe, Missouri 63369
www.bankofoldmonroe.com
Assets: $317 million

Loans: $179 million
Deposits: $259 million
Loan to deposit ratio: 69%
Profitability: average
Nonperforming loans as a percent of assets: 0.25%
Loan-loss reserves as a percent of nonperforming loans: 745%
Equity as a percent of assets: 14%

Home Exchange Bank
220 South Broadway
Jamesport, Missouri 64648
www.bankheb.com
Assets: $142 million
Loans: $55 million
Deposits: $95 million
Loan to deposit ratio: 58%
Profitability: highly profitable
Nonperforming loans as a percent of assets: 0.27%
Loan-loss reserves as a percent of nonperforming loans: 1,016%
Equity as a percent of assets: 12%

Maries County Bank
4th and Main
Vienna, Missouri 65582
www.mariescountybank.com
Assets: $451 million
Loans: $248 million
Deposits: $375 million
Loan to deposit ratio: 66%
Profitability: slightly below average
Nonperforming loans as a percent of assets: 0.52%
Loan-loss reserves as a percent of nonperforming loans: 426%
Equity as a percent of assets: 14%

Mercantile Bank of Louisiana, Missouri

222 Georgia Street
Louisiana, Missouri 63353
www.mercbk.com
Assets: $107 million
Loans: $59 million
Deposits: $77 million
Loan to deposit ratio: 76%
Profitability: Slightly below average
Nonperforming loans as a percent of assets: 0.03%
Loan-loss reserves as a percent of nonperforming loans: 6,330%
Equity as a percent of assets: 22%

Northeast Missouri State Bank
600 South Baltimore
Kirksville, Missouri 63501
www.northeastmissouristatebank.com
Assets: $105 million
Loans: $41 million
Deposits: $90 million
Loan to deposit ratio: 46%
Profitability: average
Nonperforming loans as a percent of assets: 0.01%
Loan-loss reserves as a percent of nonperforming loans: 7,890%
Equity as a percent of assets: 13%

MONTANA

First State Bank of Shelby
320 Main Street
Shelby, Montana 59474
www.fsbshelby.com
Assets: $132 million
Loans: $22 million
Deposits: $105 million

Loan to deposit ratio: 21%
Profitability: Slightly below average
Nonperforming loans as a percent of assets: 0.12%
Loan-loss reserves as a percent of nonperforming loans: 724%
Equity as a percent of assets: 20%

NEBRASKA

Auburn State Bank
1212 J Street
Auburn, Nebraska 68305
www.auburnstatebank.com
Assets: $171 million
Loans: $83 million
Deposits: $142 million
Loan to deposit ratio: 59%
Profitability: average
Nonperforming loans as a percent of assets: 0.28
Loan-loss reserves as a percent of nonperforming loans: 183%
Equity as a percent of assets: 14%

Heritage Bank
110 East 9th Street
Wood River, Nebraska 68883
www.bankonheritage.com
Assets: $594 million
Loans: $216 million
Deposits: $48 million
Loan to deposit ratio: 49%
Profitability: average
Nonperforming loans as a percent of assets: 0.13%
Loan-loss reserves as a percent of nonperforming loans: 528%
Equity as a percent of assets: 16%

Homestead Bank
915 Meridian Avenue
Cozad, Nebraska 69130
www.homesteadbank.com
Assets: $247 million
Loans: $159 million
Deposits: $208 million
Loan to deposit ratio: 76%
Profitability: above average
Nonperforming loans as a percent of assets: 0.11%
Loan-loss reserves as a percent of nonperforming loans: 640%
Equity as a percent of assets: 13%

Minden Exchange Bank & Trust Company
448 North Minden Avenue
Minden, Nebraska 68959
www.mindenexchange.com
Assets: $157 million
Loans: $77 million
Deposits: $116 million
Loan to deposit ratio: 66%
Profitability: average
Nonperforming loans as a percent of assets: 0.00%
Loan-loss reserves as a percent of nonperforming loans: not applicable
Equity as a percent of assets: 15%

NEVADA

Bank of George
9115 West Russell Road, Suite 110
Las Vegas, Nevada 89148
www.bankofgeorge.com
Assets: $149 million
Loans: $98 million

Deposits: $120 million
Loan to deposit ratio: 77%
Profitability: Extremely highly profitable
Nonperforming loans as a percent of assets: 0.00%
Loan-loss reserves as a percent of nonperforming loans: Not applicable
Equity as a percent of assets: 14%

NEW JERSEY

Somerset Savings Bank, SLA
220 West Union Avenue
Bound Brook, New Jersey 08805
www.somersetsavings.com
Assets: $566 million
Loans: $245 million
Deposits: $454 million
Loan to deposit ratio: 54%
Profitability: extremely below average
Nonperforming loans as a percent of assets: 0.03%
Loan-loss reserves as a percent of nonperforming loans: 437%
Equity as a percent of assets: 19%

NEW MEXICO

Centinel Bank of Taos
512 Paseo Del Pueblo Sur
Taos, New Mexico 87571
www.centinelbank.com
Assets: $214 million
Loans: $82 million
Deposits: $192 million
Loan to deposit ratio: 43%

Profitability: nicely above average
Nonperforming loans as a percent of assets: 0.00%
Loan-loss reserves as a percent of nonperforming loans: not applicable
Equity as a percent of assets: 9%

Citizens Bank
500 West Broadway
Farmington, New Mexico 87401
www.cbnm.com
Assets: $730 million
Loans: $204 million
Deposits: $599 million
Loan to deposit ratio: 34%
Profitability: nicely above average
Nonperforming loans as a percent of assets: 0.11%
Loan-loss reserves as a percent of nonperforming loans: 482%
Equity as a percent of assets: 10%

Citizens Bank of Las Cruces
505 S. Main Street, Loretto Center #5
Las Cruces, New Mexico 88004
www.citizenslc.com
Assets: $511 million
Loans: $271 million
Deposits: $458 million
Loan to deposit ratio: 59%
Profitability: highly profitable
Nonperforming loans as a percent of assets: 0.13%
Loan-loss reserves as a percent of nonperforming loans: 4,619%
Equity as a percent of assets: 10%

First American Bank
303 West Main Street
Artesia, New Mexico 88211

www.firstamb.net
Assets: $1,101 million
Loans: $576 million
Deposits: $961 million
Loan to deposit ratio: 62%
Profitability: above average
Nonperforming loans as a percent of assets: 0.34%
Loan-loss reserves as a percent of nonperforming loans: 1,871%
Equity as a percent of assets: 14%

First National Bank
414 10th Street
Alamogordo, New Mexico 88310
www.fnb4u.com
Assets: $329 million
Loans: $139 million
Deposits: $287 million
Loan to deposit ratio: 49%
Profitability: slightly above average
Nonperforming loans as a percent of assets: 0.08%
Loan-loss reserves as a percent of nonperforming loans: 1,641%
Equity as a percent of assets: 12%

First New Mexico Bank
300 S. Gold Avenue
Deming, New Mexico 88030
www.firstnewmexicobank.com
Assets: $213 million
Loans: $74 million
Deposits: $186 million
Loan to deposit ratio: 40%
Profitability: average
Nonperforming loans as a percent of assets: 0.55%
Loan-loss reserves as a percent of nonperforming loans: 279%
Equity as a percent of assets: 12%

First New Mexico Bank, Las Cruces
3000 East Lohman Avenue
Las Cruces, New Mexico 88011
www.firstnewmexicobanklc.com
Assets: $126 million
Loans: $53 million
Deposits: $108 million
Loan to deposit ratio: 49%
Profitability: average
Nonperforming loans as a percent of assets: 0.10%
Loan-loss reserves as a percent of nonperforming loans: 2,263%
Equity as a percent of assets: 12%

NEW YORK

East Bank National Association
183 Centre Street
New York, New York 10013
www.eastbank-na.com
Assets: $187 million
Loans: $109 million
Deposits: $151 million
Loan to deposit ratio: 72%
Profitability: well below average
Nonperforming loans as a percent of assets: 0.00 %
Loan-loss reserves as a percent of nonperforming loans: not applicable
Equity as a percent of assets: 17%

NORTH DAKOTA

Bank of Tioga
7 North Main Street
Tioga, North Dakota 58852

Assets: $295 million
Loans: $60 million
Deposits: $264 million
Loan to deposit ratio: 23%
Profitability: highly profitable
Nonperforming loans as a percent of assets: 0.00 %
Loan-loss reserves as a percent of nonperforming loans: not applicable
Equity as a percent of assets: 10%

Dakota Community Bank & Trust, National Association
609 Main Street
Hebron, North Dakota 58638
www.dakotacommunitybank.com
Assets: $769 million
Loans: $483 million
Deposits: $683 million
Loan to deposit ratio: 71%
Profitability: highly profitable
Nonperforming loans as a percent of assets: 0.17%
Loan-loss reserves as a percent of nonperforming loans: 543%
Equity as a percent of assets: 9%

Sargent County Bank
331 Main Street South
Forman, North Dakota 58032
www.sargentcountybank.com
Assets: $120 million
Loans: $54 million
Deposits: $97 million
Loan to deposit ratio: 55%
Profitability: above average
Nonperforming loans as a percent of assets: 0.10%
Loan-loss reserves as a percent of nonperforming loans: 229%
Equity as a percent of assets: 15%

OHIO

Citizens Bank Company
5th Street & Ullman Street
Beverly, Ohio 45715
www.thecitizens.com
Assets: $189 million
Loans: $106 million
Deposits: $163 million
Loan to deposit ratio: 65%
Profitability: average profitability
Nonperforming loans as a percent of assets: 0.07%
Loan-loss reserves as a percent of nonperforming loans: 1,695%
Equity as a percent of assets: 13%

First Bank of Ohio
175 S. Washington Street
Tiffin, Ohio 44883
www.firstbankofohio.com
Assets: $171 million
Loans: $81 million
Deposits: $106 million
Loan to deposit ratio: 58%
Profitability: below average
Nonperforming loans as a percent of assets: 0.30%
Loan-loss reserves as a percent of nonperforming loans: 321%
Equity as a percent of assets: 12%

OKLAHOMA

Bank of the Panhandle
1223 North Main Street

Guymon, Oklahoma 73942
www.bopguymon.com
Assets: $143 million
Loans: $80 million
Deposits: $ 116 million
Loan to deposit ratio: 69%
Profitability: above average
Nonperforming loans as a percent of assets: 0.02%
Loan-loss reserves as a percent of nonperforming loans: 3,434%
Equity as a percent of assets: 12%

Farmers and Merchants National Bank of Fairview
312 North Main Street
Fairview, Oklahoma 73737
www.fairviewbank.com
Assets: $103 million
Loans: $37 million
Deposits: $86 million
Loan to deposit ratio: 43%
Profitability: above average
Nonperforming loans as a percent of assets: 0.03%
Loan-loss reserves as a percent of nonperforming loans: 2,594%
Equity as a percent of assets: 13%

Farmers Exchange Bank
419 South Grand
Cherokee, Oklahoma 73728
www.farmereb.com
Assets: $332 million
Loans: $231 million
Deposits: $296 million
Loan to deposit ratio: 78%
Profitability: very highly profitable
Nonperforming loans as a percent of assets: 0.29
Loan-loss reserves as a percent of nonperforming loans: 888%

Equity as a percent of assets: 9%

First Bank & Trust Company
401 N. Seventh Street
Perry, Oklahoma 73077
www.bankfbt.com
Assets: $152 million
Loans: $80 million
Deposits: $133 million
Loan to deposit ratio: 64%
Profitability: above average
Nonperforming loans as a percent of assets: 0.18%
Loan-loss reserves as a percent of nonperforming loans: 832%
Equity as a percent of assets: 12%

First National Bank and Trust, Elk City, Oklahoma
2714 West 3rd Street
Elk City, Oklahoma 73648
www.fnbec.com
Assets: $320 million
Loans: $193 million
Deposits: $284 million
Loan to deposit ratio: 68%
Profitability: nicely above average
Nonperforming loans as a percent of assets: 0.34%
Loan-loss reserves as a percent of nonperforming loans: 280%
Equity as a percent of assets: 11%

First State Bank
102 West Main Street
Anadarko, Oklahoma 73005
www.fsbanadarko.com
Assets: $101 million
Loans: $20 million
Deposits: $86 million

Loan to deposit ratio: 24%
Profitability: slightly below average
Nonperforming loans as a percent of assets: 0.25%
Loan-loss reserves as a percent of nonperforming loans: 283%
Equity as a percent of assets: 14%

FSNB, National Association
1420 West Lee Boulevard
Lawton, Oklahoma 73501
www.fsnb.com
Assets: $379 million
Loans: $114 million
Deposits: $311 million
Loan to deposit ratio: 37%
Profitability: very highly profitable
Nonperforming loans as a percent of assets: 0.14%
Loan-loss reserves as a percent of nonperforming loans: 1,367%
Equity as a percent of assets: 14%

Sooner State Bank
2 Southeast Fourth
Tuttle, Oklahoma 73089
www.soonerstatebank.com
Assets: $191 million
Loans: $117 million
Deposits: $168 million
Loan to deposit ratio: 70%
Profitability: above average
Nonperforming loans as a percent of assets: 0.11%
Loan-loss reserves as a percent of nonperforming loans: 562%
Equity as a percent of assets: 12%

OREGON

Pioneer Trust Bank, National Association
109 Commercial Street Northeast
Salem, Oregon 97301
www.pioneertrustbank.com
Assets: $424 million
Loans: $281 million
Deposits: $373 million
Loan to deposit ratio: 75%
Profitability: nicely above average
Nonperforming loans as a percent of assets: 0.04%
Loan-loss reserves as a percent of nonperforming loans: 2,852%
Equity as a percent of assets: 11%

PENNSYLVANIA

Commercial Bank & Trust of PA
900 Ligonier Street
Latrobe, Pennsylvania 15650
www.cnbthebankonline.com
Assets: $386 million
Loans: $181 million
Deposits: $308 million
Loan to deposit ratio: 59%
Profitability: average
Nonperforming loans as a percent of assets: 0.18 %
Loan-loss reserves as a percent of nonperforming loans: 233%
Equity as a percent of assets: 15%

Haverford Trust Company
100 Matsonford Road
Radnor, Pennsylvania 19087
www.haverfordquality.com
Assets: $113 million
Loans: $67 million

Deposits: $88 million
Loan to deposit ratio: 77%
Profitability: extraordinarily highly profitable
Nonperforming loans as a percent of assets: 0.00%
Loan-loss reserves as a percent of nonperforming loans: not applicable
Equity as a percent of assets: 17%

SOUTH DAKOTA

Commercial State Bank of Wagner
204 South Main Street
Wagner, South Dakota 57380
www.commercialstate.com
Assets: $152 million
Loans: $96 million
Deposits: $130 million
Loan to deposit ratio: 74%
Profitability: highly profitable
Nonperforming loans as a percent of assets: 0.20%
Loan-loss reserves as a percent of nonperforming loans: 395%
Equity as a percent of assets: 11%

First National Bank in Philip
103 East Oak Street
Philip, South Dakota 57567
www.fnbphilip.com
Assets: $248 million
Loans: $164 million
Deposits: $216 million
Loan to deposit ratio: 76%
Profitability: nicely above average
Nonperforming loans as a percent of assets: 0.00%
Loan-loss reserves as a percent of nonperforming loans: not applicable
Equity as a percent of assets: 12%

First Premier Bank
601 South Minnesota Avenue
Sioux Falls, South Dakota 57104
www.firstpremier.com
Assets: $1,977 million
Loans: $906 million
Deposits: $1,717 million
Loan to deposit ratio: 53%
Profitability: above average
Nonperforming loans as a percent of assets: 0.12%
Loan-loss reserves as a percent of nonperforming loans: 744%
Equity as a percent of assets: 12%

Security National Bank of South Dakota
325 Dakota Dunes Blvd.
Dakota Dunes, South Dakota 57049
www.snbonline.com
Assets: $182 million
Loans: $94 million
Deposits: $157 million
Loan to deposit ratio: 60%
Profitability: above average
Nonperforming loans as a percent of assets: 0.03%
Loan-loss reserves as a percent of nonperforming loans: 3,644%
Equity as a percent of assets: 10%

TENNESSEE

CBBC Bank
330 E. Broadway
Maryville, Tennessee 37802
www.cbbcbank.com
Assets: $333 million

Loans: $164 million
Deposits: $275 million
Loan to deposit ratio: 60%
Profitability: slightly below average
Nonperforming loans as a percent of assets: 0.07%
Loan-loss reserves as a percent of nonperforming loans: 2,124%
Equity as a percent of assets: 17%

Truxton Trust Company
4525 Harding Road
Nashville, Tennessee 37205
www.truxtontrust.com
Assets: $412 million
Loans: $259 million
Deposits: $350 million
Loan to deposit ratio: 74%
Profitability: above average
Nonperforming loans as a percent of assets: 0.00%
Loan-loss reserves as a percent of nonperforming loans: not applicable
Equity as a percent of assets: 10%

TEXAS

Bank of DeSoto, National Association
2011 N. Hampton Road
Desoto, Texas 75115
www.bankdesoto.com
Assets: $195 million
Loans: $98 million
Deposits: $175 million
Loan to deposit ratio: 56%
Profitability: above average
Nonperforming loans as a percent of assets: 0.88%
Loan-loss reserves as a percent of nonperforming loans: $327 million

Equity as a percent of assets: 10%

City National Bank
500 N. 4th
Wills Point, Texas 75169
www.bankatcnb.bank
Assets: $137 million
Loans: $75 million
Deposits: $122 million
Loan to deposit ratio: 62%
Profitability: nicely above average
Nonperforming loans as a percent of assets: 0.00%
Loan-loss reserves as a percent of nonperforming loans: not applicable
Equity as a percent of assets: 11%

Commercial National Bank of Brady
105 E. 2nd Street
Brady, Texas 76825
www.cnbbrady.com
Assets: $165 million
Loans: $74 million
Deposits: $146 million
Loan to deposit ratio: 51%
Profitability: above average
Nonperforming loans as a percent of assets: 0.07%
Loan-loss reserves as a percent of nonperforming loans: 1,832%
Equity as a percent of assets: 11%

First National Bank
729 W. 7th
Spearman, Texas 79081
www.fnbhome.bank
Assets: $204 million
Loans: $121 million
Deposits: $167 million

Loan to deposit ratio: 72%
Profitability: above average
Nonperforming loans as a percent of assets: 0.29%
Loan-loss reserves as a percent of nonperforming loans: 319%
Equity as a percent of assets: 12%

First National Bank of Albany/Breckenridge
100 South Main Street
Albany, Texas 76430
www.fnbab.com
Assets: $513 million
Loans: $244 million
Deposits: $447 million
Loan to deposit ratio: 55%
Profitability: above average
Nonperforming loans as a percent of assets: 0.23%
Loan-loss reserves as a percent of nonperforming loans: 426%
Equity as a percent of assets: 12%

First National Bank of Hughes Springs
505 East First Street
Hughes Springs, Texas 75656
www.fnbhs.com
Assets: $252 million
Loans: $163 million
Deposits: $215 million
Loan to deposit ratio: 76%
Profitability: nicely above average
Nonperforming loans as a percent of assets: 0.22%
Loan-loss reserves as a percent of nonperforming loans: 550%
Equity as a percent of assets: 15%

First National Bank of Livingston
2121 Hwy 190 West
Livingston, Texas 77351

www.fnblivingston.com
Assets: $359 million
Loans: $117 million
Deposits: $305 million
Loan to deposit ratio: 38%
Profitability: average
Nonperforming loans as a percent of assets: 0.12%
Loan-loss reserves as a percent of nonperforming loans: 476%
Equity as a percent of assets: 15%

First State Bank
1526 Fourth Street
Graham, Texas 76450
www.fsbgraham.com
Assets: $146 million
Loans: $84 million
Deposits: $117 million
Loan to deposit ratio: 72%
Profitability: nicely above average
Nonperforming loans as a percent of assets: 0.22%
Loan-loss reserves as a percent of nonperforming loans: 334%
Equity as a percent of assets: 9%

First State Bank of Ben Wheeler, Texas
14269 State Hwy 64
Ben Wheeler, Texas 75754
www.fsbbenwheeler.com
Assets: $135 million
Loans: $66 million
Deposits: $118 million
Loan to deposit ratio: 56%
Profitability: above average
Nonperforming loans as a percent of assets: 0.09%
Loan-loss reserves as a percent of nonperforming loans: 659%
Equity as a percent of assets: 13%

First State Bank of Burnet
136 E. Washington
Burnet, Texas 78611
www.fsbburnet.com
Assets: $256 million
Loans: $64 million
Deposits: $224 million
Loan to deposit ratio: 28%
Profitability: slightly above average
Nonperforming loans as a percent of assets: 0.10%
Loan-loss reserves as a percent of nonperforming loans: 1,079%
Equity as a percent of assets: 13%

First United Bank
201 N. Broadway
Dimmitt, Texas 79027
www.firstunited.net
Assets: $1,116 million
Loans: $710 million
Deposits: $937 million
Loan to deposit ratio: 76%
Profitability: above average
Nonperforming loans as a percent of assets: 0.13%
Loan-loss reserves as a percent of nonperforming loans: 766%
Equity as a percent of assets: 12%

Frontier Bank of Texas
1213 Highway 290
Elgin, Texas 78621
www.frontierbankoftexas.com
Assets: $147 million
Loans: $89 million
Deposits: $119 million
Loan to deposit ratio: 74%

Profitability: below average
Nonperforming loans as a percent of assets: 0.07%
Loan-loss reserves as a percent of nonperforming loans: 464%
Equity as a percent of assets: 18%

Industry State Bank
16886 Fordtran Boulevard
Industry, Texas 78944
www.isbtx.com
Assets: $703 million
Loans: $138 million
Deposits: $615 million
Loan to deposit ratio: 22%
Profitability: above average
Nonperforming loans as a percent of assets: 0.05%
Loan-loss reserves as a percent of nonperforming loans: 1,792%
Equity as a percent of assets: 12%

Inter National Bank
1801 S. 2nd Street
McAllen, Texas 78503
www.inbweb.com
Assets: $1,843 million
Loans: $938 million
Deposits: $1,385 million
Loan to deposit ratio: 68%
Profitability: below average
Nonperforming loans as a percent of assets: 0.47%
Loan-loss reserves as a percent of nonperforming loans: 380%
Equity as a percent of assets: 25%

Mason Bank
111 Westmoreland Street
Mason, Texas 76856
www.masonbank.com

Assets: $111 million
Loans: $38 million
Deposits: $85 million
Loan to deposit ratio: 45%
Profitability: average
Nonperforming loans as a percent of assets: 0.12%
Loan-loss reserves as a percent of nonperforming loans: 595%
Equity as a percent of assets: 17%

Muenster State Bank
201 North Main Street
Muenster, Texas 76252
www.msbtx.com
Assets: $168 million
Loans: $34 million
Deposits: $134 million
Loan to deposit ratio: 26%
Profitability: slightly above average
Nonperforming loans as a percent of assets: 0.00%
Loan-loss reserves as a percent of nonperforming loans: not applicable
Equity as a percent of assets: 15%

Sanger Bank
501 North Stemmons
Sanger, Texas 76266
www.sangerbank.com
Assets: $131 million
Loans: $70 million
Deposits: $114 million
Loan to deposit ratio: 61%
Profitability: average
Nonperforming loans as a percent of assets: 0.09%
Loan-loss reserves as a percent of nonperforming loans: 592%
Equity as a percent of assets: 13%

SOUTH CAROLINA

Palmetto State Bank
601 First Street W.
Hampton, South Carolina 29924
www.palmettostatebank.com
Assets: $528 million
Loans: $180 million
Deposits: $434 million
Loan to deposit ratio: 42%
Profitability: average
Nonperforming loans as a percent of assets: 0.30%
Loan-loss reserves as a percent of nonperforming loans: 598%
Equity as a percent of assets: 15%

UTAH

Optum Bank, Inc.
2525 Lake Park Boulevard
Salt Lake City, Utah 84120
www.optumbank.com
Assets: $5,042 million
Loans: $447 million
Deposits: $4,170 million
Loan to deposit ratio: 11%
Profitability: nicely above average
Nonperforming loans as a percent of assets: 0.04%
Loan-loss reserves as a percent of nonperforming loans: 238%
Equity as a percent of assets: 10%

VIRGINIA

Farmers Bank, Windsor VA
50 East Windsor Boulevard
Windsor, Virginia 23487
www.farmersbankva.com
Assets: $415 million
Loans: $243 million
Deposits: $335 million
Loan to deposit ratio: 73%
Profitability: average
Nonperforming loans as a percent of assets: 0.41%
Loan-loss reserves as a percent of nonperforming loans: 895%
Equity as a percent of assets: 12%

WASHINGTON

Cashmere Valley Bank
117 Aplets Way
Cashmere, Washington 96815
www.cashmerevalleybank.com
Assets: $1,392 million
Loans: $838 million
Deposits: $1,212 million
Loan to deposit ratio: 69%
Profitability: slightly above average
Nonperforming loans as a percent of assets: 0.07%
Loan-loss reserves as a percent of nonperforming loans: 1,364%
Equity as a percent of assets: 11%

WEST VIRGINIA

Bank of Monroe
39 Main Street
Union, West Virginia 24983

www.bomwv.com
Assets: $126 million
Loans: $60 million
Deposits: $106 million
Loan to deposit ratio: 56%
Profitability: average
Nonperforming loans as a percent of assets: 0.20%
Loan-loss reserves as a percent of nonperforming loans: 346%
Equity as a percent of assets: 15%

WISCONSIN

Farmers State Bank of Waupaca
112 West Fulton Street
Waupaca, Wisconsin 54981
www.fsbwaupaca.com
Assets: $178 million
Loans: $94 million
Deposits: $149 million
Loan to deposit ratio: 0.63%
Profitability: average
Nonperforming loans as a percent of assets: 0.27%
Loan-loss reserves as a percent of nonperforming loans: 549%
Equity as a percent of assets: 15%

First Citizens State Bank
207 West Main Street
Whitewater, Wisconsin 53190
www.firstcitizensww.com
Assets: $301 million
Loans: $161 million
Deposits: $240 million
Loan to deposit ratio: 67%
Profitability: slightly below average
Nonperforming loans as a percent of assets: 0.05 %

Loan-loss reserves as a percent of nonperforming loans: 1,375%
Equity as a percent of assets: 18%

National Exchange Bank and Trust
130 South Main Street
Fond du Lac, Wisconsin 54936
www.nebat.com
Assets: $1,381 million
Loans: $731 million
Deposits: $1,057 million
Loan to deposit ratio: 69%
Profitability: average
Nonperforming loans as a percent of assets: 0.35%
Loan-loss reserves as a percent of nonperforming loans: 585%
Equity as a percent of assets: 20%

Nekoosa Port Edwards State Bank
405 Market Street
Nekoosa, Wisconsin 54457
www.npesb.com
Assets: $213 million
Loans: $117 million
Deposits: $184 million
Loan to deposit ratio: 64%
Profitability: average
Nonperforming loans as a percent of assets: 0.39%
Loan-loss reserves as a percent of nonperforming loans: 365%
Equity as a percent of assets: 13%

Shell Lake State Bank
102 5th Avenue
Shell Lake, Wisconsin 54871
www.shelllakestatebank.com
Assets: $178 million
Loans: $74 million

Deposits: $139 million
Loan to deposit ratio: 53%
Profitability: slightly below average
Nonperforming loans as a percent of assets: 0.18%
Loan-loss reserves as a percent of nonperforming loans: 534%
Equity as a percent of assets: 19%

CONCLUSION

No one can guarantee that every bank listed in this book will survive the next financial crisis (and in my opinion there will definitely be one). But based on their performance statistics, these banks will have a much better chance of weathering such a storm.

There are, of course, other factors to consider in choosing a bank: Customer service high among them. Location was a paramount issue in the long-gone pre-Internet banking days, and still may be for some, but for most people, after an initial meeting and getting your accounts set up, there is little reason to have to go to your bank today.

I have written this book with the purpose of informing readers about the precarious condition of the domestic and even international banking scene. And to provide them with information that will help them make the best banking choices for themselves, their families and their businesses. And in so doing protect their assets and help them prosper.

I hope you found the information interesting and useful.

If you want to stay informed on matters of banking, finance, and investing, you can subscribe to my financial newsletter *Strategic Financial Intelligence* (**https://www.strategicfinancialintelligence.com**).

Meanwhile...

Keep your powder dry.

John Truman Wolfe.